MARCIA YOL

Searching for

LOVE

in all the

WRONG PLACES

ISBN 978-0-9951827-1-4

Printed in Canada

TABLE OF CONTENTS

FORWARD

....

By all accounts, Marcia Ford should not be amongst us today. However, by the grace of God, she is here today, to share with us her story of strength, determination, and perseverance against what seemed like insurmountable odds.

Have you ever faced adversity, bemoaned what your next move will be? Have you lost faith in yourself and the Lord, and began searching for love in all the wrong places? Marcia has, and she will inspire you with her tenacity and drive to find her way back.

Born on the sunny island of Jamaica, and lacking nothing of the material world, Marcia begins her search for what was missing in her life, a father figure. From a tiny island to this immense land her life changes in unexpected ways upon her arrival to Canada.

Pregnant and unwed, Marcia faces the struggles and judgments as many teenage mothers do but with an added factor, she was sent to Canada to study, not throw her life away, as was thought by many.

Read on as Marcia recounts her time with her stepfather, to searching the streets of Montego Bay as a 14yr old looking for her father, only to be sadly rejected. Follow as she begins life in Canada and discovers whom she really is and was meant to be. From that scared and confused seventeen-year-old child to a wife, mother, minister, entrepreneur, speaker, and philanthropist. I invite you to take the time to read and follow Marcia's journey it will empower you to persevere, to live life on your own terms and realize your dreams. "One woman can move a mountain if it is in her way."

Forward by: Deborah Ferdinand,
Editor and Writer – Creative Consulting Services

DEDICATION

....

T o my family and friends, thank you for taking this journey with me and blessed be to God for giving me the strength and guiding me through this life, my life.

One of my many reasons why I wanted to write this book was to share my experiences with you. Where I was, may be where you are; how I arrived at where I am, may help you map your journey. I hope to inspire you and motivate you to believe in yourself.

I dedicate this book to my children Joema, Yolanda, Jermain, Jeremy and, Orethea, and to my mother Myrtle Agatha Rowe.

....

The inspiration to write this book come from my personal life experiences and the conviction that was laid upon my heart to share my story. This book as been in the work for over ten years but somehow I just could not find my way to complete it and get it to you. Two years ago to date, my story would not let me go. I finally made up my mind and began to write searching for love in all the wrong places. We all find ourselves searching for something in some way shape or form .I have always believed that this book will change lives and make a difference in today's world.

....

WHERE I WAS

By the spring of 1997, I was a pregnant seventeen-year-old, a new immigrant to Canada and by the fall of 1998, I was married to Oreth.

This was a confusing and very difficult time for me, as it would be for any young girl. Yes, I was still a girl, a girl that was certainly misunderstood by most everyone in my life.

Imagine being introduced to someone for the first time, and they have drawn their own conclusions about you, they have judged you based on what they have heard and their own biases without knowing you. As a seventeen-year-old and a member of the Jamaican community, every 'auntie' felt it was their right and obligation to express their opinions and along with that right, comes criticism. This is a lot to bear for a young girl; I am filled with worry, fear, and feelings of uncertainty for my future. I wondered how I got here, where do I go from here? I felt very alone, it felt at that time that I was the only person in the world with this weight to carry and no one wanted to understand me.

Now do not feel sorry for me, sure there is a lot of underlying hurt that just does not go away. It can hurt for years to come and I feel and know your pain. I also believe my pain, past, and present has helped me to overcome adversity. We hurt often at times because we lack the ability and know how to overcome our present situation and may feel trapped. I hope reading this book will leave you with words of wisdom and some guidance to help you overcome the storms of life while walking with your head held high.

As humans we strive to be happy, seek companionship and love, it is in our nature. The average person does not wish to be unhappy, alone or unloved, but sometimes these situations are thrust upon us. I learned that when you are alone that is when you truly know who you are, this is also the time you find out how solid you are, are you going to come out standing stronger?

Finding your place in the world and peace in your heart is something we all should strive for; and when you have found that peace only then can you navigate your way through an ever-changing world. Our lives are shaped by our genetics, environment, and experiences; quite often as these factors influence our lives, they change and shape who we are. Sometimes you may be unaware of the change and how you see yourself in a mirror may not be how others see you.

*"Do you see what I see
what you see
what I see."*

Marcia Yolanda Ford

Few of us can take an honest look in a mirror at ourselves and accept or change whom we are; and it is only when you are comfortable and accepting of what you see, will you then realize what others see when they look at you. We are also quick to see only the physical, your nose, lips legs etc, its easy to see the flesh but hard to see who you are and what God has ordained for you.

Teenage pregnancy is a reality and is life altering. For some it may feel like a death sentence, your dreams are placed on hold, you may have to make some very adult decisions, you feel lost.

I am here to tell you that there is hope; there is that light at the end of the tunnel. Read on as I share with my story of where I came from and how I came to be where

I am. I hope it will inspire and motivate you to get where

you need to be, finding peace and happiness in your life.

....

ONE

AS I BEGAN

One may ask why, how does one search for love in all the wrong places. This may seem inconceivable to some. Often times we will build walls and don't know how to remove them, and sometimes circumstances build prison walls for us, it may be your family or the ones we love the most. Gold is tested with fire to assure its authenticity, we as human are also tested every day. How you break down those walls and triumph through life is the test of your mettle.

Sometimes we search for love in education, in our jobs, in a man, sex, drugs, or sometimes we have the great desire to search for love in all the wrong places.

For example, some study for quite a long time trying to fill that void that will not just go away, from high school to college and then university, some are even studying further on. Studying is not bad I am just shedding light on the fact that sometimes we are searching and we do not even know it. Do you know anyone that studies all his or her life and never had a job? On the other hand, can never keep a job with all the education they have. That is someone who is searching for something.

Let us talk about that one person who can command your attention by the way they look at you, the way they hold you, and just by the tone of their voice your brain freezes, you are unable to think. The intense desire that passionate expression of love can hold you even trap you for a very long time in a world built just for you, and you stay waiting for the next high. In that moment of ecstasy, you will believe everything and anything this man tells you, he can do no wrong in your eyes. If an angel were to fall from the sky and tell you anything different from what you were feeling, you would respond with words that are not fit for the ears of angels or man. How do we allow one person to have such a hold on us? You dream every day of how to break down these walls; some saying you are crazy to stay. However, we all must pass through this passage at some point in time and we have to find our way back. Understanding how we are loved by the creator:

For God so loved the world, He gave us His only begotten Son.

John 3:16

Moreover, when we forget, our walk sometimes goes from one bed to another, boyfriend to boyfriend again journey to journey. We lose weight and gain weight because we are searching for love in all the wrong places.

....

TWO

AS I FIND MY WAY

U nderstanding oneself is the beginning of one's journey, as I grew up not understanding my life and myself; it was difficult to make sense of the negative as well as the positive events in my life.

Please join me as I relate to you how I found my way in this world.

My journey begins at the age of nine, I lived with my older siblings Janet and Monica and Garnet my brother in Kingston. By this time in my life, my mother was living and working in Trelawny Parish and my sisters Janet and Monica are caring for Garnet and me. I remember this time fondly even with the spankings, that time in my life holds some of my fondest memories. At the same time, I did not understand the meaning of love.

I mastered the art of cooking acquired cleaning skills but never mastered the laundry; hated it! Garnet would wash my clothes for me, then put them back in the basin so my sisters would believe I did a good job laundering, ah the fun we had. Ah, it did spare me from a spanking! As kids, we had it all, a roof over our heads, money coming in, food, and clothes but we knew nothing of affection, gentle ways or kind words.

It began when a pot of water spilled onto my right thigh as I was sterilizing my niece, Dania's baby bottle. My sisters got me to the hospital for medical attention and all was fine with my injury and recovery. My mom did not know of the burn or trip to the hospital, there was no way of reaching her. When my mom finally came to visit she found out that my sisters did not give me a chance to heal, my chores, cooking, cleaning, and laundry continued. At that point, my mother made the decision to take and my brother and I back with her to Trelawny Parish. As a kid, the thought of going to the country was exciting, and there was a sense of peace in my spirit. I did not recognize it as that, I was just 10 years old, I just knew I would be away from my sisters and maybe I can get some love and affection from my mother. My journey begins in December 1991 in South Trelawny Jamaica.

My mom taught us that hard work pays off all the time. I learned the concept of work very early in life; you can achieve what you want in life if you work hard and smart. My mother was not a believer in a formal education, she was not the best reader or writer and she was ok with that. She felt it has not interfered with her life and she sees nothing wrong if you cannot read or write. In spite of her beliefs, she sent me to school.

My mother was an entrepreneur; she owned a large business in the market trading food, we had a nice and respectable store. I helped my mother in the store, you could say that I was the head and brains and she was the hands and feet of the business, I loved the role I was given.

One could say my entrepreneur skills were born, the business was doing well, and life was good for some time, despite my mother working non-stop.

Being privileged children, we had a helper that looked after the house and took care of Garnet and myself, she made sure we went to school and that our general needs were satisfied. She must have had a difficult time my brother and I were always in fights at school, you talk too hard it coming! Some of my fondest memories, would be when mom would cook a whole chicken for my brother and me, mom does not eat chicken! More for me, as kids, we loved our food, and as for me, food was something I did not like to share, surprisingly I love to entertain today and share, how I have changed.

My mom made sure all our material needs were taken care of, we could eat and drink as much as we wanted; my brother and I were the envy of all the kids in our community. I wanted for nothing but had nothing. That love, that warmth and that sense of belonging were not there; it was almost a perfect upbringing until Mackenzie came along then everything changed overnight.

It was not until Mackenzie came into my life that I really knew and experienced true emotional upheaval. He was determined to sever what little affection and love my brother and I received from my mother and showed no mind to how much damage he was causing.

He did not like my brother and me, this was very evident, he had children of his own and we were not his. As children, we did not understand why mom was having this man move into our house. The atmosphere in the house became very tense, but mom made sure we ate and had clothes, and as a kid that is all I cared about, how soon that changed.

Mackenzie's plan to break apart our family centered on 'carrying news' about me and my brother. He told stories of how we gave away merchandise from the store, who we spoke to in the day and our comings and goings. There was no way two twelve and fourteen kids could defend or explain themselves to a mother who was blinded by love. There is a very old question, 'why would a mother choose a man over her children?' There are multiple reasons and answers, but the result of Mackenzie's meddling was a wall built between mother and children.

Everything that God blessed us with was no longer sweet it was all bitter. Garnet and I began acting out, and as a result, we were spanked. We both began running away from home regularly, and with the parish being small, it was easy for mom to find us.

We were unable to express ourselves, and the pain became too much to bear for any child, we had no outlet or way to express our feelings, fears or desires. The pain just kept growing inside. As young teens, we were having a hard enough time getting adjusted to growing up, as all young adolescents do; rebellion, speaking out, and relation-ship, it's all a part of growing up. Having to live with stress and feeling deep emotional rejection in the place that was supposed to be your refuge, is not a part of growing up, and was too much to bear.

As kids we were always thinking of ways to exclude Mackenzie, in our heads maybe he would leave if things were not good. Because of my love of food, I felt that most everybody else valued it as I did. We began cooking enough food for three, mom, Garnet and me. We would wash the dishes and clean up the kitchen and made sure to put food aside for mom, and for my stepfather we made and left no food for him.

It was our simple way of gaining control over a situation that was filled with uncertainty and doubt. Life did not improve, our tricks did not work, and mom paid no mind to us, her children. We were suffering, we did not know how to express what we were feeling, and much less, we could not understand the situation that our mother had placed us in. When you hold a human being's emotions hostage, sometimes the result can be frightening.

Mother's take care not to tune out your children when they are crying out for help open your ears and heart so that you can help. Today many children fail because no one will hear them, no one takes the time to read their facial expressions, or notice the tone in their voice or their body language, and sometimes we miss seeing their pain.

As an adult when we experience emotional pain we are sometimes lost for words, you have a hard time expressing and processing your feelings. Now think of 12 and

14-year-old kids having to navigate through these rough seas of emotions with no support and guidance.

Do you remember I said we had all these tricks and plans to get Mackenzie out of our lives? Garnet and I decided that we would kill him; yes as unwise as it sounds to you, we believed that it was our only way out. We went as far as digging a grave. Foolish children do foolish things. After some more plans and thought, we realised that we were kids and could not pull off such an act, if only for a lack of inexperience!

I am thanking God we did not know how to kill him because we would only now have been released from prison for killing that man. God had angels guiding me and my brother, to do the right thing, not hurt another human being. However, that pain shaped my life in so many ways, that pain that hatred that seeps into my spirit and soul and takes a hold of me.

THREE

....

CHANGES ONCE AGAIN

Time passed I was now 15 years old, the pain was still there, and so was Mackenzie. As my situation goes from bad to worse, my emotional scars got deeper and deeper as each year passes. The only way I knew how to deal with my feelings of pain was to act out, how else was I to be noticed, get attention, or get love. I now discover boys and my world turns upside down! This thing called love is about to take me on a rollercoaster ride, some big highs and lows to come. From the age of 15 to 22, I started looking for someone to say I love you too and to hear those words said to me. I fell hard for anyone who would show me affection or give me the attention I so desperately wanted.

I did not grow up with a father or father figure and so I sought the love of my father, Carlton Ford. Therefore, what was a young girl to do, I went searching for love, searching for my father. I was by this time very good at running away and planning. The Confidences bus passes through my neighbourhood once a day and could get me to Montego Bay. I formulated my plan and being a kid I told all my friends what crazy scheme I was up to, so it was very easy for my mother to find me, but not before I met Carlton Ford.

I made my way to Montego Bay and began walking the streets of Green-Pan district asking people if they knew Carlton Ford. Once again, God's angels were looking after me; I met some women who heard that I was looking for Carlton Ford and saw the resemblance in my face. I was taken to meet him and at first he denied that he was my father, eventually, he was called out as a liar by my aunt, the resemblance was too strong to deny paternity. I was not well received by Mr. Ford. I was the product of his extramarital affair with my mother. He had money and power and I would disrupt his world. He gave the usual promises, I will come to visit you, I will not forget you, that was 25 years ago, and I am still waiting. I often tell myself I do not need him, and it meant nothing to me, little did I know that this meeting and longing for a father was going to shape my emotions positively and negatively for some years to come. I often long for my father's presence and his love, the chance to know and have him in my life.

As I began in earnest my search for love, I encountered a tall and beautiful black man and as beautiful as he was on the outside he was beautiful on the inside. He understood me and knew what I wanted. However he did not return my love and was man enough to tell me that I did not know about what I was speaking of, this thing called love. I was always ready to say I love you; the meaning of this word to me was to find comfort in something or someone. Clive was older and wiser he understood my naive youth. We often use this word so lightly, without knowing the consequence of what we saying, or even what it means. Love can be a feeling, the way he looks at you, or he provides for you, for some of us this is how we define love, for others, there is no definition, just a drive to find love in whatever form or definition of love that comes along.

Some people sell their souls all in search for this love. There is an unexplained void, which will not go away it will keep you searching, and trying to fill that space. For many, a high keeps you coming back for more. Others feel that peace of mind, but sometimes you can be fooled into that false sense of security; that as long as you are in the arms of your lover you are at peace.

Oftentimes this behavior does take a toll on us because we now place our hope in others and give over our rights. We put everything in the hands of others, because of a love and trust we have for them.

If you are an inventor of a product would you hand over your formula to me to do as I please with it? No! Then why in our everyday walk we take our heart, lives, and happiness, place it in the hands of others and expect that person to treat you with the same love you have for yourself. Consider if you do not love yourself, how do you expect to be loved? Only when you master that art of how to love yourself, then that is the time you will find this the peace that surpasses all understanding of love.

I was so lost in my own world that I did not see that my search was taking me down some dark paths and I had to learn eventually how to light my own way. I now know that every experience is there to build your character no matter how bad or how good it is.

My sister Janette was always saying to me, the world is not going to end tomorrow, you will get your share of the pie, and that I should continue my studies, as I grew older. She told me that I would be able to choose which man I would want to live my life with. Her belief was once you have an education your life's position will change and as a result, your views would change as well, but all that she said fell on deaf ears. I just thought this world was going to end and I would not see the age I am today, all this from the mind of a confused and lost child.

It all comes back to trust and building a strong communication line between yourself and your children. I cannot express how important it is to reach out to our children while they are still innocent. Janette reached out to me but it was too late my innocence was nowhere present, I had been on this wild ride for so long and no one understood or would even take the time to understand me and with that they all gave up on me. Words do hurt; they have an impact on your self-esteem and your belief system. There was the lady in the community that said nothing good can become of me, it was a very hurtful statement and for some time in my life I lived that limiting belief that nothing good can become of me.

There were only three teachers that took the time to work with me and was able to see the potential in me, Miss Powell, Miss B.Gagne and Miss Hutchinson, they planted a seed in me. The seed did not take root then but as the seasons passed, it grew and grew to the realization that I can accomplish something great with my life.

As I think back, I feel bless hearing that nothing good would every come of me, this was a motivating tool for me, it never left my memory and I always told myself I will prove them wrong and I did just that with all the negative I have learnt to turn it into a positive.

The year is 1995 and my mom always tells me you are

going to Canada, I just could not understand why I had to go, I did not want to go but that was what I was told would happen; she wanted a better life for me. Monica my eldest sister would be the one sponsoring me to migrate to Canada.

April 9, 1997, that day arrived. I felt God had great plans for me in Jamaica; I was still bewildered as to why I was to move so far away, to Canada. So many thoughts went through my head, was it because I was always fighting? I was so much of a runner; instead, I learnt how to run, was it that. Was it in my behaviour in my desperate search to find love in all the wrong places?

....

FOUR

AS I PASS THIS WAY

I was seventeen-years-old when I arrived in Canada to live with my sister Monica. Imagine coming from my small town to Toronto; the first thing that really caught my eyes were the skyscrapers. The first words out of my mouth when I saw those tall buildings were, how could I own one of those? Everyone just laughed at me. As far as I was concerned, it was not a joke, why were they laughing. Looking up at the skyscrapers the thought came to me, I can do all things with God if I believe.

Three weeks into my new life, new opportunities, a

chance to start over, and hold my head high; I was being registered for school. Now, my joy was short lived and I was going to find out just how strong I truly needed to be. When the time came for me to get registered for school I began feeling nauseous and I soon discovered I was pregnant What was I to do, the father, Oreth was in Jamaica, I was seventeen years old in a new country, but in hostile territory. This news carried home to my mother very quickly, she was disappointed in me because this trip was to change my life for the better. You remember that mirror; few of us can take an honest look in a mirror at ourselves, I was not one. I felt there was nothing wrong with me; I do not need to change environments or change myself. I felt that God had big plans for me.

At the request of my sister and family, I was told terminate the pregnancy or go back home to Jamaica, I refused and my challenge got worse. I was headstrong and steadfast in keeping my pregnancy; there were constant battles with my family. I chose to marry Oreth in 1998 at home in Jamaica. The twins, yes twins were born Jermain and Jeremy and the long process of sponsoring their father began.

God kept me safe; he sent the right help at the right time, friends like Tyrone, Prince, and Mr. Spencer. Had it not been for these angels I would have lost my mind. They entered my life at a time I needed support, not opposition. I realise that people will come into your life for a time a reason or a season and I was and still am very blessed to have them in my life. Just like this book, you are reading this at the right time and place and for the right reason, and I will offer you hope and inspire you to make that journey and own your skyscraper.

October 2004 was an awakening moment for me; I realized that I had been living in a hazy dream for eight years. I awoke from what seemed like a dream but was not a dream. The Lord allowed me to see my life from high above; as I looked down I saw where I was, married with five children and a husband. I had been absent for so long. I could hear my sister's voice advising me but no one was there. I tried to wake up and realized it was not a dream, I am here in this world and I do not even know how I got here, alone and out of favour with my family and in-laws. I needed to talk to someone to express myself as I raise five children in a new country. When there is little to no communication between people, there is no understanding and empathy for each other, that is how misinterpretations and quarrels begin. There was a lot of misunderstanding, a misreading of body language, and the tone in our voices, this is not to say that I do not like my family, the opposite is true, I love and treasure my family. I know that the past can make or break us, but my experiences and my 17-year journey to find me have shaped me into the powerhouse of a woman I am today, with God's grace.

FIVE

....

WHAT A RIDE

I made a choice to have my twins, but youth and the lack of life experiences did not prepare me for how difficult my life was going to be. The twins came early, as it can be with teen pregnancies, but I wasted no time getting my life back on track.

I applied to George Brown College as an independent student and passed the entrance exam; I studied for one year and four months and graduated with honors and at the top of my class as a personal support worker. My diploma was instrumental in shaping my life to this day.

I was still lost but slowly finding my way.

As I tried to find my way I experienced one of the darkest moments in my life; everyone was not who they appeared to be, I was being let down by the people I trusted and my life was harder than I ever dreamed. Little did I know that this was to be one of many dark moments in my life. I put myself on a one-way street, a street that was moving forward not backward, up the escalator searching for something, was it love or myself?

I had one of the most heart-wrenching experiences a woman could endure. I saw my world in a certain way and others had not see it as I did, and this in itself was depressing and traumatizing. My heart hurt like it never had before. I would give anything to remove my heart from my chest; the emotional pain was such a physical pain as well. I was confused; nothing made sense in my life at this point, there was no one there and it was as if I was the only one in this world carrying this weight.

I was working overnight at St. Michael's hospital in 2002, and while sitting in a rocking chair resting on my lunch break I felt a warm sensation come over my body, it was the feeling of being shrouded in warmth. God came into that lunchroom and offered me comfort and hope, I cried and was lost for words; in that moment my peace was restored. With that knowing and belief that God loves me, I was able to pick myself up and move on the only way I knew how. According to scriptures, if you can dream it you can have it.

Where there is no vision, the people perish: but he that keepeth the law, happy is he.

Proverb 29:18

Speaking it makes all the difference.

Death and life are in the power of the tongue: and they that love it shall eat the fruit thereof.

Proverbs 18:21.

Those who love to talk about others carry gossip or spew negative words will reap the consequences of their words and actions. If you choose to do the opposite, use your tongue to spread love and positivity, you will walk in the light and what you speak will be projected in your life. If you can dream it you can have it, and speaking it makes all the difference. It took me some time to come to the realization I needed to vocalize it, own it and believe in my dreams. God presented me with many rivers to cross, I was beginning to understand my relationship with God, and his plan for me.

You may recall the old nursery rhyme, which was derived from Psalm 42:10 Sticks and stone may break my bones but words will never hurt me. Words almost bent me to the ground; it was as if those words were sticks and stones. I chose not to have it break me but I chose to stand strong.

We often fail in this game called love; we look for love in others and become disappointed and sometimes angry when love is not reciprocated. If we take the time to understand that, a man or anyone for that matter just cannot give what they don't possess, especially if they don't love themselves. If someone does not value him or herself or have a standard that they live by, how is that person going to give you what you want, when the reality is that to who you look is locked in the same situation as yourself? God reminds us that if a man is not being led by God then he is being led by something or someone else. The graveyard is filled with many dreams, hopes, and what-ifs.

God lights the way; we must walk in the light of God. We all have a destiny to fulfill and I believe that I am here for one reason, to walk on the path God has set out for me and it will lead me to fulfill the destiny through God.

As I asked myself, I now ask you, are you capable of overcoming your past? Are you ready to create new footprints in the sand?

....

SIX

TAKING INVENTORY

Have you ever taken the time from your busy life just to sit and meditate on your life, your journey? Do you know or sense what destiny the Lord has laid out for you? Do you know what footprints you will leave in the sand? I believe that God puts you on a path to enlightenment and love. It may seem as if there are many rivers to cross, mountains to climb and adversity around every corner. The Lord does not set us up for failure. There is a reason for everything and at times, we must face those challenges to see the light of the

Lord God. We are all here for a reason, there is a purpose to our lives, and   staying on the path will guide you to your purpose here on earth.

My question to you, have you discovered your purpose, do you know why you are here and why you experience life the way you do?

Meditate on the following questions, take a deep look at yourself and be honest with yourself, see where you are on your life journey.

Do you feel as if you lacking or missing something in your life?

Do you feel as if you need to go searching for that something missing?

Do you know what you are looking for?

Have you been hurt by someone?

Do you feel scorned?

*For in him dwells all the fullness
of the Godhead bodily and ye are
complete in him, who is the head
of all principality and power.*

Colossians 2:9–10

He gives and he takes, open your heart and ask yourself, what do I see?

I will tell you what I see when looking into my heart; I see promise, love, hope, vision and dreams. I know that God will do me no harm or inflict pain upon me and all his promises for me will come to life. You may not realize this but your heart is your road map to life. You are royalty, a child of the King. Do you know the power that our God has placed in you?

Take some time to search your soul.

Is it well with your soul and how do you know?

Is your soul well?

Is your soul happy?

How do you know if it is well?

Do you have peace and feel at peace?

If you are not at peace do you know why?

Do you know how to find this peace?

What is the formula?

Have you discovered or experienced love?

....

SEVEN

YOUR TONGUE IS A READY INK

M y heart is overflowing with a good matter: I speak of the things, which I have made concerning the king: my tongue is the pen of a ready scribe.

Your tongue is a ready ink it can paint a bright picture or a bleak picture of your life, your words can shape the lives of the ones you love.

Psalm 45:1

Did you know that stress is linked to the six leading causes of death? Not everyone, however, can handle stress in their lives, which can result in depression; some of us turn to professionals for help, and others take a darker path of alcohol, drugs, or sex.

I am responsible for all my actions, so I built my world around my family despite our differences and disagreements. Managing all my responsibilities on my own was not an option and I owned my decisions and actions. In order to move forward, I had to wear many faces, I kept my feelings of stress, disappointment and loneliness well masked, I needed to stay strong and focused in order to set a new foundation for my life and that of my children. At the time, I did not know what foundation I was building, but instinctively I knew it was there all the time, our Lord Jesus Christ. By relying on our Lord I was able to learn how to use the resources that the Lord gave to me and I was happily surprised at how richly I was rewarded with the endless love and peace I was blessed with.

Staying strong and focused every minute of your day is difficult and my life was compounded by external stress as well. There was a day in 2004 when I did not know if I was coming or going, I was in such a dark place that I felt the only way out was to take my life. I felt that the pressure was too much to bear, those masks that I wore were fooling my family and friends, and they did not know I was in such a dark place.

Some of us unconsciously inflict this pain upon ourselves, I did. I made choices but I was still refusing to take full responsibility for my choices. I looked at everyone else as the source of my pain and I failed to look in the mirror at myself. I began searching for peace and I felt that if I kept focusing on my involvement in the Lord and my church, I would weather the storms.

It was not enough that I carried a personal burden, why would my place of refuge, my church not embrace me. I chose to become very involved in my church's ministries; from singing in the choir, tea socials, youth groups and attending services on a regular and frequent basis. After some time, I became uneasy and distracted, these were familiar feelings and they resonated from the feelings of rejection and hurt. As I sat in service, I felt I was there in body but absent in mind and when I was there in mind I was absent in spirit, what was distracting me, what was pulling me away from my time with the Lord. As I tried to make sense of my feelings, I began to review my role in my church. The church regularly called on me to provide the cooking and baking for church events, all free of charge, the ingredients, the presentation and my time. Why is it that my church has the funds to pay for all events, and when the funds are depleted they approach me to cook and provide food free. Is that the only time I am of value to the church? I wondered, #mummyforhelp.

That was a game changer for me, I felt that I was being

disrespected and being taken advantage of. In 2005, those feelings were back; I felt as if I was under attack. I lacked self-awareness of my situation, I wanted to fit in and from looking in from the outside, it seemed as if I did fit in. However, my mask hid the fact that I was still very lost inside, my heart and soul were aching. I was torn, between the church and my own spiritual health, I had many sleepless nights not knowing what to do, and how do I go about fitting in. You could say I was searching for a sense of purpose.

I once again found myself in a place where I just did not know what to do with myself, work is stressful, my home life is stressful and now going to church is stressful. I was beside myself. I felt ostracised, disliked and not accepted by my fellow parishioners. Little did I know that all I needed to sustain my spirit I have inside of me, but that would take some time for me to unlock.

In my wisdom, I thought it best to take some time away

from the church, regroup my thoughts and decide how I will handle my feelings and the situation. I called on my friend Prince and asked him to take me out to a club so I can DJ some music. From church to club, I was simply crying out for help and looking for love, still wearing one of my many masks, no one knew of my turmoil. At the club, I felt loved. This was the feeling I wanted from my church, so with a false sense of love, I decided to abandon the church.

As I began to sing, a woman shouted out that my voice was made for the church, not the club. Some would say that I was very confused and clearly chasing something, with those words I returned to the church as if nothing had happened. The emotional pain was still there, and would only get worst. There came a day when I began to see the light of hope and understanding. My church had a visiting Preacher and he reminded me that when God calls you, it is not just 'a' call but instead a qualified call, he knows what specific task he has set out for you and God believes that you will succeed. He went on to say that we each have a destiny and purpose in this life, and King Jehovah knew me before I was in my mother's womb and he knew the number of hair strands on my head.

Many are the plans in a person's heart, but it is the Lord's purpose that prevails.

Proverbs 19:21

But I have raised you up for this very purpose, that I might show you my power and that my name might be proclaimed in all the earth.

Exodus 9:16

With those words, I felt I had begun to understand more of the love Jesus Christ has for me. I was learning from every disappointment I had endured, and every time I felt I could no longer go on, and the only good constant in my life was Jesus Christ.

As I continue on my journey to finding me, I realized that my past has held me in bondage not through the actions of others but from my own actions. Again, I was reminded that I have to own up to my actions.

I came to realisation that I had been using sex to deal with my life's problems. I was fooling myself saying that I am in love, each time. Looking back how could I have not seen that it was not love but instead passionate sex?

....

EIGHT

NO MORE BONDAGE

I lacked the knowledge to interpret the scriptures on my own, but in that moment, I understood the Lord's language. It took prayer and fasting and divine intervention to understand what God was saying to me, if we were not in his presence, we would not understand his message. God says that experience teaches wisdom and without experience, how can we teach and help others. I believe that we must all go through trials and it is through these trials that we are tested and it is only then you will have a testimony. God gave us perfect minds, body, and soul and I order to receive his gifts we must be prepared.

Why do we often beg God for help, and when we receive that help, we are sometimes unprepared? When I ask the Lord for help, I must be ready to receive, because the power is in my tongue. I asked and I received in more.

Have you even noticed that the priceless stones are never found lying on the side of the road? In order to find these stones, you have to dig and sometimes you have to dive under the water to find them, as God's children we are more precious than stones or gems and sometimes buried so deep, it takes some time to uncover this rare gem. Moreover, we are God's priceless stone.

In November 2005 God was about to fix me. I was in a dream state and saw myself receiving a blood transfusion. I was under a very bright light, there were doctors operating on me, and I felt as if I were in that room for some time. They were replacing my heart and other organs and I sensed there was a lot of work to be done. My organs were shutting down and I heard the doctor say 'I had to replace every organ in your body, they were all infected, and your body is still shutting down.

Part way through my dream I noticed a tube attached to the left side of my body that led outside, I could not see where it led to so I decided to follow it. To my shock, I saw someone drawing the blood out of me through the tube. God revealed to me who it was and I awoke in dumb silence and was even more confused, my King revealed to me what ailed me. Sometimes when you ask for help, it arrives in a form you did not expect and sometimes that request turns out to be a hard truth. I asked the Lord for help thinking it would arrive in the form of something tangible, a better environment, a better job all things that I felt would better my situation. Instead, I received a message of awakening. It is very difficult to see the truth about oneself and if we cannot handle the truth, denial sets in and this can lead to mental illness. I said to the Lord, no this could not be true how can this be?

*Search me, O God, and know
my heart, try me, and know my
thoughts: And see if there be any
wicked way in me, and lead me in
the way everlasting.*

Psalm 130:22-23

To get to the root of any behavior or situation you must take a long hard look inside of yourself and when you find the root cause only then can you have deliverance.

I say before you, your deliverance is locked inside of you, and it is only a matter of unlocking it.

*Why do we search? It is because
of a void that will not go away,
and only the love of God can fill
that void. Many people search
because of the lust of the flesh*

and sometimes the flesh takes up predominant residency, and we always feed our earthly vessel. Therefore, brothers, we have an obligation, but it is not to the flesh, to live according to it.

Romans 8:12

There is no waiting and no tomorrow for this flesh because the flesh knows no limit to wanting and questioning. Have you ever loved someone, gave them your all, and in the end you are still wanting more? That is your flesh, it wants food, sex, and does not know how to say no to indulgences. However, your flesh says no to fasting, praying, and respecting your body, with diet and exercise, which will help with clarity of mind.

God had revealed to me what was locked in my dreams, I was lost for words and refused to accept what was revealed to me, and denial took root. I returned to prayer, I told God you have shown me a mystery, and I demand a clearer understanding of this dream. However, the picture was very clear but I was not willing to accept it, so I quarried God for some time believing that the answers would change, just for me. Could God have made a mistake; this message was not intended for me?

There are times we ask God for favors but we lack the patience to wait and because of that lack of patience, we take what was not handed to us. Later on at the height of your life when nothing makes sense, we ask God why. Most times, we are not ready for the answer he gives us, and often we cannot accept the truth. Until we can accept and live the truth we will never have that breakthrough we so long for.

As God speaks to me in my dream, he reminds me that if he did not have me in the palm of his hand I would be dead or have lost my mind. He points out how I felt no pain during the operation, and from this day forward, I will feel no pain, my veins flowing with anesthetics-pain killers. Once I awoke, I was able to interpret my dream clearly.

I realized that the heartache would not go away because the pain was more than I could handle and for some time I believed I would not make it. I knew I needed to change my mindset. A major influence on our daily walk through life is our mindset and to be able to understand the season, the time in your life, and the reason why.

"The mind can be a field of flowers or a cage of pain, if we lack the ability to process the information that is being downloaded or if your processor is outdated."

Marcia Yolanda Ford

My new mindset was adopted and I came to the

realisation that I was no longer feeling stressed, not much bothered me, the past was the past. I fared well for some time, I was handling the difficulties of life fairly well, I knew there would always be a silver lining to my problems and this was a part of my daily walk through life.

....

NINE

NOT MANY DAYS SINCE

J uly 8, 2009, my world would rock once again, I received a phone call telling me my brother Garnet had been shot and has died. I was in a good place in my life and I could not understand, why, why again, and I was about to find out how deep and rooted I was in my beliefs. I have lost other family members, but never a sibling. I now stood in a world of grief that I have often spoken of but never experienced myself. For four years, I worked in Palliative Care and thought I knew it all about death and dying, so I thought. Due to the fact that Garnet was shot, there were many mouths ready with a negative comment without knowing all the details, I needed words to sustain me not weaken my heart. My brother passed away by being in the wrong place, at the wrong time, it was his appointment time with the Lord, and no one else could keep that date but Garnet. He was killed by what I believe to be a corrupt police force in Jamaica, as much as we tried to seek justice for Garnet, no witnesses were willing to come forward for fear of police retaliation.

I do not know how I would have made it through this trying time if it were not for the words of encouragement and empowerment from my friend, Clive.

Now I began to question myself, what could I have done to change what had happened. Did I do my best for him, did I spend enough time with him, and did I really know him. I had come to Canada at seventeen and I knew that the bond was not as tight as it should have been. Nevertheless, he was my only brother and I loved him.

The pain of losing Garnet was compounded on the day of his funeral; I came to the sad realisation that I will never see him again. The memories came rushing back and my heart began to hurt all over again. My brother always liked extra gravy on his food, and I never noticed the same in my children until after Garnet was gone, I now take comfort and smile in memory of my brother for each request for extra gravy. Nothing worried Hussy; he was able to adjust easily to new environments and situations and was always smiling, laughing and making jokes.

As I looked at the face of my brother in his casket, he seemed to be in a peaceful sleep, and I wanted to call to him, 'Hussy, Hussy' and he would wake up. I knew that could not be thus making it harder for me to accept his passing. I wanted Garnet to wake up and to see him smile at me and begin laughing for no reason, but Hussy was gone; my heart and spirit were broken.

As the months pass my emotions are still fragile, but

life has some changes in store for me. I began being introduced to an artist and radio station hosts and I thought of Garnet, he loved music and his only dream was to make it big someday as a singer or DJ that was Garnet's passion.

Despite meeting all these individuals, I was still in pain. As children Garnet and I loved music, we would get into trouble for going to Ninja Corner in Seaview Garden to compete in live DJ competitions, winning all the time. Garnet was very good at sing-offs, DJ and concerts, unfortunately, we had no one to help promote him, at that time I was not connected with anyone in a position to help. Today, I am well connected and if given the chance I would help Garnet succeed today.

Life is filled with irony, God, where were these people in high places when we needed a break, as kids! In retrospect we were not ready we were lacking in so many ways.

Only after the death of Garnet in 2009 was I now in a position to reach all the right people. As strange as it may seem to you, all this success, the pain was still there on every level, I could not share my joy with my brother. God does know best and as time passed, it became easier.

R.I.P: Garnett Mendaze (aka Hussy) - Sunrise June 14, 1976, Sunset July 8, 2009.

....

TEN

PROJECT CIRCUMSTANCES

I had been a member of my church since 2000 and when Garnet passed in 2009, I felt ignored by my brothers and sisters, I felt like a visitor; they treated my brother's death as if he was just an acquaintance of mine rather than my family. I needed their support and prayers, nothing had changed, it was like how it was before, I was an afterthought. By the time the church decided to acknowledge my circumstances, it was too late. The hurt and rejection I felt from my Church were too much and all the hurt started rushing in, I decided not to return to that Church.

I was in a very interesting place, this new rejection left me bitter. Some of us may go through some hurtful situations, and it may not be easy if you hold on to bitterness for many years. I chose to pray to get past the hurt and bitterness, but I refused to attend any organized religion. For six months, I stayed and prayed at home, I told myself never again; never will I give to any organization and then complain in my heart.

With that decision, I decided to develop my own charity as a way of giving back and helping my community. Initially, I was not able to register as a non-profit but I did not let the paperwork and red tape slowed me down, but I continued pushing forward with my decision.

Project Circumstances was born on October 9, 2010, I began by hosting a kid's fun day in Allside District and making sure each child received a gift. To ensure this project was a success I implored the help of Miss Nicketa and Miss Kimi, and over time they helped bring the events to life. With the help of these two angels, I was able to realise another dream in April 2011.

Little did I know that when Miss Green and Kimi came on board that our journeys would be so intertwined. Kimi is like a mother, albeit younger than I am, cooking and making sure I ate, 'Sue you beta eat come and eat' she would say.

Nicketa would make sure all the finances were in order and this played an important role in launching Sue Yen Sue Place.

There were others who supported my projects, and to those individuals, I am very grateful. However, a special mention to Nicketa and Kimi for being there rain or shine, lending their support and guidance, angels who helped carry me through. Miss Green, Kimi, and Laz, a friend and a rock that God sent to help me stand. Good friends are very hard to find and when you find them you must always take care of them, you may never know how God will use the people in your life to bless you. God will use those persons to bless you in a way you could never imagine and when it happens, you will be left with doors that are open. No one but God is instrumental in opening those doors and no one can close those doors until God deemed so. At all times be careful how you treat others, at any given time you could be encountering angels and unaware that those individuals will be the tools and avenue God uses to bless and change your life in so many ways. Time will pass and they will become a part of you, as family and there will be nothing you cannot accomplish with their help and support.

One year after my brother passed away life started changing for the positive. I purchased a piece of land in Jamaica and was ready to build Sue Yen Sue Place, where I would be providing services and jobs in the community, this was my way of giving back and honoring my brother's memory. The only dark spot was that Garnet was not here to share these moments with me.

The next face of my life saw individuals who began, as strangers become friends and family. Nicketa and Kimi entered my life and bless it, they became family and helped me to walk on a path I had never ventured on.

ELEVEN

EGLINTON AND JANE

January 17, 2004, I experienced a day I will never forget, the day I gave birth to Yolanda and almost lost my life. I went into labor and I was bleeding and alone at home with four other children. Somehow, I believed that if I called 911 emergencies for help they would come and take my children away, I think they call that 'pregnancy fog'. Another wise decision I made was to put all four children in the car and drive to my sister in Toronto. This was not a very thought out plan, there was 14 centimeters of snow on the ground; I had to drive from Brampton to Toronto, and then drive myself to the hospital. The pain was unbearable, the driving conditions were dangerous, the children are crying, my contractions are five minutes apart and I was still one hour away from my destination. As I drove I implored God to keep us safe and help get us to our destination. To this day, I remember that moment clearly, as if it were yesterday as. I approached the intersection of Eglinton and Jane, I am now a bit more at ease, and my sister's home is near, a left turn to get to my sister's home. The road was very slippery and covered in centimeters of snow, as I made that left turn I began to lose control of my van; the van was sliding and did not come to a stop. As a 40-foot trailer was coming towards us, I shouted Jesus and Jesus took the wheel from my hands, the trailer missed us and the van came to a stop. Despite our near brush with death, I had to pull myself together and continue on my way. After leaving the children with my nieces, I continued on to Humber River Hospital, there were miles to go but I keep on going, the pain was excruciating. I kept a mantra going, 'I shall live and not die, I will be ok I know this is not the end, I will see many days come.' From my vantage point, things looked bleak, but I continued to believe and pray that the Lord would see me through, still not knowing where I was receiving the strength.

When I arrived at the emergency entrance I was so weak and disoriented I did not know if I was coming or going. I remember clearly, I did not park my car, a man assisted me from my car into the hospital and I thank God I made it, I believed that I was going to be okay. I was in a fragile state; any new emotionally trauma was a setback.

Once I got to the maternity ward my emotional war and pain began, I remember the nurses as being ruff. I would imagine considering the state of emotional and physical distress that I was in, the nurses had a hard time with me, 'pregnancy fog'. I was 23 years old with four children, every nurse felt it was their obligation to berate me for being young pregnant. They were saying things like, open your legs, it was sweet when you were doing it so be ready to enjoy. I was feeling like fish out of the water. The contractions were steady and minutes apart, and in that moment I believed that I would not make it to see another day. A mother dying during childbirth is not uncommon, and for a split moment, I thought I would be next. I believe that the time I spent praying, while I still had my faculties, was instrumental in carrying me through one of the most painful experiences of my life.

Has your heart ever hurt so much that you believed that you were going to die? The thought of removing your heart from your chest seemed like your only option at that moment. My day begun with labor pains, my water breaking, bleeding, fourteen centimeters of snow, four babies in the back seats and a harrowing trip to my sister's and then on to the hospital. My day, January 17 ended with the

Lord keeping me safe for another day and an opportunity to be his disciple and testified.

....

TWELVE

GOD KEPT ME

On the journey through life, you have some experience that leave you saying, why me Lord? This was just one of those experiences, sometimes you have to walk through broken seashells to get to the water, an ouch experience.

I was working as a youth services worker, the pay was good and I got on well with my co-workers, so I thought. I worked closely with my supervisor and after some time we developed a friendship. I love to travel and feel out of sorts if I stay still for too long, I had an opportunity to go to New York City for the long weekend. My supervisor verbally granted me the time off and suggested that I take an extra day off to recuperate after my trip; never would I have thought this would be used against me.

I did not realise my supervisor had grown attracted to me, he began making advances towards me and I would put him in his place. Despite his behavior, we were friends. He invited me out to dinner and I had to remind him that he is married, but I still saw him as a joke, and I declined his invitation. Because I would not entertain his lust for me, he used the extra day off he offered me as his ace in the hole. He proceeded to inform the head office that I refused to show up for my shift, and that is how I lost my job at the home. I was angry and upset; I did not know what to do, or how to fight this decision. I took his flirtations and passes to lightly, and I did not have proof. I believed he was my friend and not just a co-worker.

Time and season pass and I began to move on.

You could say I landed my dream job next at Community Living. With ten years experience in my past job I learned some things about people, some of it not very nice, and with this experience, I arrived well prepared for my new job, the people and the work environment.

My shift was two weeks of day shifts and two weeks of night shifts and with a family of five young babies, this was a perfect arrangement for saving money with baby-sitters. This job was very important to my family and me but being resourceful, I kept a small catering business and an ongoing hair product project that I could work into my schedule. I cannot sit still for too long, so I resigned myself to working day and night.

I will always stand up for what is right and report an incident if it deems to be reported. There was a woman I worked with who always had something to say about everything and everyone and it rarely was truthful, she was ever afraid to challenge what she observed. This woman told me that she saw a staff member hitting a resident. I did not witness the incident and I was unsure of its source, so I thought I would investigate it myself before reporting it, I did not want someone to lose their job with unjust cause. I checked with the individual and saw no evidence of abuse. Before a 24-hour period was up I was called to the office and I was the one who lost my job. In those few minutes I paid a price for someone else's trouble, I was bitter and just could not understand why.

You cannot be liked or get along with everyone and it is true that not everyone is going to like or get along with me. It could be as simple as not liking the clothes I wear the tone in my voice or my demeanor; these are some of the things that give rise to misunderstandings. When you possess multiple skills, you put yourself out there as a target for those who thrive on negativity and they will do things to pull you down or go further ad have you fired.

This type of fear stems from feelings of insecurities and lack of self-esteem and belief in yourself. I choose to be happy for others and myself.

I did not understand, my past experiences taught me to keep my guard up, I did not understand how I let my guard down in this situation?

I was exposed to running a business at a young age in Jamaica, entrepreneurship was in my blood. I made it a part of my regular conversation to talk about my ventures and learn more about entrepreneurship. Marcia's Cake and Catering Service came about in 2011-2012, and I was very proud of my business. What puzzled me were the pointed questions people would ask me, "how do you run a business if you work full-time, why do you even work the government can support you, and if you're working so much, how come you are not rich?" These people chose to question my drive and abilities, by casting doubt on what I was doing. My trust and belief in man were to shake me again; little did I know that this jealousy and envy would be a source of trouble. Some felt that if they had the skills and talents that I do, they would never work again. Well, that is not me.

I have been blessed with abilities that surpass my understanding some days. I do know what holds true, the Master knows best, he knows why he gives and takes away and why he builds us up only to break us down. Yes, I can say that I am truly bless in so many ways.

When God created me he provided me with the talents and skills I need to survive, I can cook, bake, decorate cakes, produce hairs products, and provide insurance, write, sing and the aptitude to make sound business decisions. That is how God made me and I do not see the need to apologize for how I have been created. God give each of us the talents, skills and abilities to thrive in his light. I did not acquire all my gifts at once or easily. I had to experience life; pain, sadness, regret, challenges, disappointment and happiness to learn and appreciate these skills. The time and season in my life dictated the reason for my trials, and from my trials, I gained strength, knowledge, and perseverance. Many see my success and glory and want to walk in my shoes, but little see or known of my pain. I am sharing this with you so you may gain some strength and understanding of your situation, yourself, and belief that life will get better.

Life's challenges are many and they affect each of us in a different way, at a different time and in varying intensities. The biggest challenge is that if you have never travelled that road before and there is no roadmap, you need to rely on the guidance, wisdom, and experience of those who have travelled that road. This book is about giving back to our youth who may come upon this road and do not have a map. We need to remind our youth that pain that could make or break you, and without sometimes falling down you cannot rise up tall and proud. There will be mountains to cross, but how we cross those mountains is the lesson we will learn and profit by. In life, there is death and a seed must die to be reborn in its true glory and full potential. Our life experiences are present not to hurt us but rather to open our eyes to the world and ourselves.

God has many molds of clay; King David, Elijah, Samuel, Nanny of the Maroons, Marcus Garvey, Maya Angelou and Martin Luther King Jr. We are made from God's design, it is up to every one of us to find our mold and embrace the gifts and graces God has bestowed upon us.

For example, the engine that runs a Ford F150 cannot adequately run a Nissan Titan. Just as human we can only reach our true potential when we are in the right vehicle; only when we address our spiritual, mental, social and physical health then and only then, will you reach your true potential.

Each of us handles stress differently, some weather it well while others shut down and may never find their way back. Your mind is a place where you do not want to get lost in daydreams and imaginations or escaping reality. Meditation can bring some balance and keep you grounded in the here and now, bringing peace and calm to a turbulent mind.

My work keeps me balanced and mastering my mind through meditation and in establishing my mindset, I can walk strong. The Bible says that it is with the mind we worship God and your mind must be clear and present, this is not easy, but with prayer and meditation, clarity can be achieved.

....

THIRTEEN

FOOD FOR THOUGHT

What is your breaking point? When do you say enough?

As I reviewed my life experiences and how they have shaped me, I realized that jealousy is poisonous. Family and friends will see you struggle and ever lend a helping hand, they may not understand, do not know how to help, or just not care at all. Now, why is it after many tears, sleepless nights and praying to God, you finally begin to achieve the graces of God, jealousy rears its ugly head. Suddenly everyone is distancing themselves from you, they are seeing and sensing a change in you before you even realize the change. Family and friends display closed body language to you, their message is loud and clear. I questioned myself, have I offended them? No, it is the spirit of jealousy. As I struggled very few people offered to lend a hand, some not knowing or perceptive enough to ask, others could not care about my circumstances, but once I acquired peace and success in my life, many wanted to share in the bounty. I am reminded of the children's folk tale of The Little Red Hen,

> *The Little Red Hen asked her barnyard friends;*
> *"Who will help me plant the seeds?"*
> *"Who will help me cut the wheat?"*
> *"Who will help me take the wheat to the mill to be ground into flour?"*
> *"Who will help me bake the bread?"*
> *To which they replied, not I.*
> *"Who will help me eat the bread?"*
> *To which they replied, I will.*

For even when we were with you, this we commanded you, that if any would not work, neither should he eat.

2 Thessalonians 3:10

It takes a toll on you to see how you are being treated and being viewed by family, friends, and co-workers; it was a depressing and emotionally challenging time as I came to grips with my emotions. I could not see what they said they saw in me and I wanted to know what they saw, all in an effort for better clarity and insight into me.

I sought support and comfort in prayer, I asked our Father to show me how I am seen by the world. What do they see when they look at me? I see no other than Marcia (Sue-Sue) Ford, a child d that God has blessed. I have an outgoing and friendly nature, I can have command of a room and from an early age, I could sense jealousy in the environment. I would not know how to change or want to change who I am; I have always been this way to the best of my knowledge. I know that I am not perfect,

but I live with taking what I see and where I am suitable me, I am adaptable. At one point in my life not too many people enjoyed spending time with me. I found myself focusing on trying to change myself to fit everyone's idea of me; I was craving a sense of belonging and searching for love in all the wrong places.

I felt like an outcast among my family and friends, but in the world of business and with my colleagues, there was no misunderstandings or misconception where my persona was concerned. It was in this world that I was able to unlock my destiny. I was embraced in a very positive way and received guidance from my business colleagues.

While spending more time with this group of business owners I now realised that there are so many different platforms and on this platform, I was understood, and accepted for who I am. I began to pray in earnest happy at this turn of events in my life. It was in prayer that my father revealed to me that I am blessed, my destiny is great and my position in life does not define me. I was told much will be given but much is required of me. As I stop to take stock and reflect on the many roads I have walked, I have to laugh to at myself.

All the same, I asked this question for some time, for seven years I tried to understand this spirit of jealousy that keeps attacking me at the beginning and at the end of all my victories. My heart is clean, I do not hold grudges but this jealousy had me in a very tight place, and each time I thought it was over it came back full circle. I have searched my heart and I know that I will forgive, but I do not easily forget to ensure that such a person would not have that opportunity again to hurt me. You will find no hostility in my heart and in my spirit.

Knowing my heart and taking this journey, I have come to realize that it will never be easy. People will always think what they want and will have their own perception of reality and until they can see another way, they will never change. It is so important to search your mind and soul and see if God is pleased with you and you are pleased with yourself. Awaken your conscience:

There is a way which seems right to a man, But its end is the way of death.

Proverbs 16:25

Sometimes, changes and this awakening happens only when your back is against the wall. It takes the realization that the person you tore down is now lifting you up and is the answer to your problem. God sometimes uses situations like this to prove a point and in doing so elevates you in the eyes of others and then they will look at you a better light.

What I have observed about the nature of humans in this time of technology, is how accessible the answer is on the web, Google. They have to see it to believe it, if Google says so then it must true, that is proof. There was a time when you said something and it meant something, such as the word of God. We have not seen the Father, but we love, believe and welcome him into our lives. Do you need Google to offer you proof of God?

If I am not careful, I will find myself in this same place. Once upon a time we went to mom and grandma for information, like cooking and cleaning and now we all go to Google. I often remind myself to keep God's remnant in my spirit and that I am able to stand in the time and season I live.

*God kept me so I would not let go.
I came close to giving up; I could
not face my problems anymore
and was bound by depression.
Jesus came into my life and keep
me grounded. God kept me so I
would not let go.*

Many people have said that I am 'strange', I have thought about this for a long time, and I cannot see this 'strange' that I am supposed to be. I gain strength in my belief that I can do all things through Christ. I learned through difficult experiences that Christ is my savior, and true assistance and guidance comes from the Lord. God will help those who help themselves and if you lean on the Lord all things will come to pass. As I pilot my ship as best as I can, I am reminded that Jehovah is my chief pilot and when I revoke his will, I am quick to return to his presence for guidance.

I am a warrior, friend, sister and, a no-nonsense person who is confident and accepting of who I am.

It has taken me a long time to understand that there is no second chance to make a first impression people will remember you the way you presented yourself. Think back on all your first times; the first time your heart raced for someone, or how your heart broke for that same someone, your first paycheque. These memories are ingrained in our memories. Such is the same for my first experience with the Lord, I prayed and asked for help, and God delivered, it was a profound and mighty experience.

That is why I say there is no second chance to make a first-time impression, you may be remembered and it may be based on a wrong impression.

You are your own reflection of what are you projecting to the world.

If you ever find yourself lost, take some time to talk to the man in the mirror and I am sure you find your way.

Self-correction is necessary, humility must be present in your daily walk and you will find that peace. When the day arrives that you find peace, all will be well.

Marcia Yolanda Ford

I was told by a very good friend that, there is no 100% guarantee in this life, and if I live my life and know that I should always leave room for the things that God will do ,and only then I will be ok.

As I passed this was searching for love in all the wrong places, I have found the never-ending love of Jesus Christ, a love that is there for all seasons, time and all reasons.

To everything there is a season and a time to every purpose under the heaven:

Ecclesiastes 3:1

....

Minister Marcia Yolanda Ford is a strong woman of faith who has transcended the many difficulties that this world has dealt her. Minster Ford is now embarking on the next stage of her mission here on this earth through the launching of her book, *Searching for Love in all the Wrong Places*.

Born on October 9, in the beautiful city of Kingston, Jamaica, Minister Ford grew up under the guidance of her elder sisters, Janette King and Monica Henry. Under her mother's wing, she learned the importance of entrepreneurship, which has proved to be a great asset in her life, and, in turn, has made her into the powerhouse that she is today.

She immigrated to Canada in April 1997, where she attended George Brown College in Toronto, Ontario and graduated a year later with honors and at the top of her class.

This was only the beginning of the great things that were in store for her in her new life in Canada. She is a licensed marriage officer in the province of Ontario under Service Ontario Canada. Over the course of time, Minister Ford also became a certified wedding cake decorator as well as certified interior decorator with a specialization in décor for weddings. She is also a fully licensed insurance representative and a developmental services worker.

Minister Ford is the founder and CEO of Sue Yen Sue Productions. On top of all of the above, she is now adding Author to the many hats that she wears with the launch of her new book, *Searching for Love in All the Wrong Places*.

In her spare time, Minister Ford enjoys relaxing by the water, seeking the face of God and bringing people together to enjoy life, no matter what current circumstances may be. She also enjoys time in the kitchen cooking and baking and is always willing to lend a helping hand to those in need. As she says, "I stand by believing that unless I have helped someone, only then have I truly lived".

She is the proud wife of Oreth for over 18 years and mother of five children.

ACKNOWLEDGEMENTS

....

Thank you for taking this journey with me, it has been a dream of mine to write this book to share my walk and experiences with you. I hope to continue sharing my experiences and insights into life within coming books.

Thank you to everyone who has been there for me, supported me and gave the strength to carry on. I could never have done this by myself. Thank you to the lord Jesus and my mother Myrtle Rowe for taking the time to nature me into the woman I am today. Emeka A.O, Laz, Toney Vanessa Thorpe, Heliu ,Mr and Mrs Testimony, I am blessed to have you in my life. My family, Oreth Joema, Yolanda, Jermain, Jeremy and, Orethea, you are my foundation. Thank you to Remi, Marlene, Sally, Rose,- Gissel Fred, and my Facebook family for always having my back and everyone that helped me on my journey.

....

*S*earching *For Love In All The Wrong Places* is a must read for anyone who has been living with the hurt, pain, guilt and a feeling of hopelessness. Marcia has done a great job in bringing awareness to issues that we have in our lives, and issues we are afraid to confront.

Thank you Marcia, for your honesty; your biography has helped me to reflect on my life's journey, recognizing that I am not alone and that there is hope in adversity.

Julie Spence

Founder, Spelling Bee of Canada

Pastor Marcia Ford has been a great inspiration to my life as a young woman and entrepreneur. While working alongside her, she has showed me through her actions, demeanor and courage to never give up, to be strong in every circumstance and to be passionate about the projects one puts their hands to. I aspire to become a great mother, business woman and motivator as she is. This book, *Searching for Love in All the Wrong Places* is a must read for every young woman - and man - who is about to begin their search to find out who they are in the world. It is a great eye opener, and through Pastor Ford's story and testimony, many hearts, minds and people will be changed.

Christina Gwira

Head Web & Mobile App Developer, NOYADESIGNS

Made in the USA
Charleston, SC
08 February 2017